Praise for *Burial Fragments*

"*Burial Fragments* is part song for the end-times, part song for San Francisco, its longtime troubling glamor and glamorous trouble. With perfect lucidity, the poems draw us into the speaker's daily anxieties—will the plane go down? will the earthquake come?— while expertly situating these anxieties within their rightful contexts—late-stage capitalism, climate crisis, the ever-present ghosts of the great fires and the AIDS pandemic. Then, in the midst of so many possible endings, there is a beginning: a child arrives. The speaker becomes a father who must negotiate his growing sense of threat even as he reads to his son: "I censor. I form a human shield./ I leave whole cities unburned." What seems at first to be a collection about psychic displacement becomes, in the end, a collection about psychic *placement*—about the ways we finally ground ourselves in the places and people we love. If you want to read a book that sugarcoats nothing, that insists on seeing things as they are and revealing who we are, read *Burial Fragments*. Keith Ekiss is a poet to turn to right now: these poems are so clear-eyed they are visionary.

—Brittany Perham, author of *Double-Portrait*

BURIAL FRAGMENTS

Published by Gunpowder Press
Edited by David Starkey and Chryss Yost
PO Box 60035
Santa Barbara, CA 93160-0035

Front cover image: Detroit Photographic Co., *Market Street, San Francisco* (1900). Library of Congress.
https://www.loc.gov/pictures/item/2015647623/

ISBN-13: 978-1-957062-21-1

Library of Congress Control Number: 2024927541

www.gunpowderpress.com

Gunpowder Press is part of Gunpowder Poetry, a 501(c)(3) nonprofit literary organization. The Barry Spacks Poetry Prize is supported in part by the Santa Barbara Poetry Fund under the auspices of the Santa Barbara Foundation.

Burial Fragments

Poems

Keith Ekiss

Gunpowder Press • Santa Barbara
2025

for Robin and Benji

CONTENTS

"Not the person only, but what's behind the person."

—Anthony Hernandez
(American Photographer)

The End

—Berkeley/Hayward fault

When the next tremor
        startles us awake
down falls the glass and ashes

the superstitious say
        we deserved it—
hidden rivers burst

toward the surface
        a disco shakes
like a waterbed strays

forage behind private doors.
        Turn off the stove,
turn off the gas, the meal is wasted.

Helicopters confirm the burning,
        guitars tune up:
tragedy needs a song.

There will be no end.
        Now we're bent
to the depths, the new death

we should've seen coming.
        Where will you go?
To your friends who collect guns

or the ones who serve gin,
        stumbling home
to sweep up your share of the wreckage?

I.

Memorial

I spot a pasted broadsheet:
Capitalism isn't working

while shops along Mission Street
sell jeans, pawned guitars, stacks

of white socks, quinceañera dresses
in confessions of pink,

corsets to cinch a bust and waist
to the modesty of prior centuries.

I watch mothers push their children in
and out—clothes for baby, in and out,

white fish from the fish monger,
black-and-white eyes

glazed like dice the small-time
gamblers roll. Small bets, simple rules:

if a throw goes cold, blame the hand
of the devil. Ones and sixes, wagers

ascending in spirals toward heaven
where St. Selena sings their fate . . .

sidewalk salesmen and dealers
of notched cards, guitar-men

who strum their secret chord.
Ones and sixes, twos and threes,

skulls and wire, desert altars
of melted candles and water bottles,

ripped shirts tied in flags—
a memorial for the newly dead

and the living who pass into the city.

Into the City

Off the train, up to Market, I discover a separate city
        of quarter films and hustlers,

veterans who wear the clothes they're given,
        mothers who awake to find the safety pins missing,

pierced into the lips of three chord punks who can't tune:
        The Very Idea of Fucking Hitler.

Dogs flash teeth like jewelry. History's written in brick
        and fracture: statues of soldiers, streets

minted with the names of robber barons.
        A dome rusts to the color of the dollar.

Once the city shook and burned.
        Now the citizens find themselves in ruins:

pink façade of a hospital through mist,
        the sick with views of the ocean and bridge.

Threat Level

       Benches meant for children
occupied by old men

clutter the playground
       and interrupt the slides
where a schizophrenic takes

interstellar dictation.
       I'm looking for a way out—
not a way down

and play the game
       of sidewalk juxtapositions:
cons versus dot coms

crazies versus kids
       in superhero shirts.
Side-eyed I watch

untrimmed hedges,
       listen for brush lurkers
if the volume of footsteps

turns up. Startle to a shriek
       of gulls. *Do you partake?*
he asks with Victorian fust.

The coast looks clear
       but I can't make it to the coast
and what would I do once I got there?

Stroller (for Harry Callahan)

Mothers pushing strollers
turn my head— in spring skirt and flats

her lumbar gap
reveals the calligraphy.

A nestled baby fights sleep, milk drunk,
covered head-to-toe in plastic

like he's caught some rare disease.
He wails, she calms.

What would it take, you wrote,
to make a city in me?

Harry always turned to Eleanor—
Eleanor on the beach

flesh tone close to sand, or breasts
shy below the water

soaking up the rhythm of the waves.
Eleanor expecting reclines in bed

posed beside a bowl of apples.
There's only the pair of us.

No leaf— only branch.
No fears at night or stories to repeat.

Panic Flight

On a plane in calm air the throat my throat
too narrow no breath.

Thought I'd faint couldn't faint.
Thought I'd drown drenched in sweat.

Our pilot hadn't issued any warning.
Other passengers didn't stir.

Wanted the trip to end suddenly
didn't care about the Prado firmly

against bullfights and all of Spain.
Until then I had only the vaguest

notion of panic the common public
nerves addressing large crowds.

Why couldn't all this begin to end?
Settled for a layover dark hotel room.

Didn't know what was happening
didn't know what had happened.

Couldn't spot the in-flight metaphor:
trapped and lost. The earth was nowhere.

I wasn't then in any kind of danger.
The plane never dipped or veered.

Projection

A careless haircut means
        there's a weapon
stuffed in the pocket of his trousers.

I pick a way through the bus
        out of bodily range
thieving my way toward safety.

Why do I think I'm the target?
        So the barber's scissors slipped,
or he cuts it himself.

How I got filthy inside I can't say,
        all shields and shivs,
digging at the anonymous.

Here, the doctor says *metaphor*.
        I'm trapped like a rat and no spring
opens on the calm and wonder of home.

*

Men pushing ice cream carts
   summon children after rain;

scents of orange blossom
   paint the neighborhood.

A city makes itself known
   corner by corner; I won't loiter

by the projects or liquor stores.
   I circle past the halfway house

and its haggard teen offenders—
   Do you see the purple flowers?

a mother asks, leading a boy
   between the known and unknown,

street men who pause from dice
   long enough to let a child pass.

*

If you step too close, I shrink
        from day as much as night:

the knife in my mind
        I place in your hand.

Now's your chance, slice the skin—
        see if tongues draw blood.

*

The man's leg looks severed
       mid-calf; I note the serge,

check twice to see if it's his foot
       gone missing or merely fabric.

Gangrene, diabetes, motorcycle spill.
       Answers float by like garbage.

I never would've thought of him again.
       Hours later at a sidewalk sale

I paw the goods: shirts, watches, jewelry.
       He's there like me, cutting deals.

Why place his face in your camera?
       You didn't think he'd see you

fingering the trinkets, believing
       there was nothing of your worth.

*

What if the subway caved
        in like a grave? I'm buried.

What if I lost my way?
        Who's pocket-lurking? Who's got

nothing to lose? The stairway
        entrance was clearly marked

and lit but I couldn't bring
        myself to walk that way.

Blam-Blam

At the corner market, one that sells cheap fuel, I heard a shot, backfire or gunfire it wasn't certain when the schizophrenic, a gas station loiterer, pointed a pistol-finger at my eye *blam-blam* and pulled the imaginary trigger. I didn't fall, didn't bleed, no one surrounded me. No gate opened, light shining through, no hands lifted me to heaven. Hold the coffin, I'm not dead. I'm an ordinary citizen. But there's a ricochet of think inside my pinball head. I like to stay in one place without moving. Let's review the tape again: no weapon was present. I want the end or the beginning not the unknown middle, the place we're always in.

The Shape of Conversation at The Gold Cane

Daniel's heroin mouth agrees with my politics. His father's money buys the beer. Daniel hasn't taken any job, he says, in years, because they don't meet his *criteria*. As the night progresses, dropping change on tips and Pabst, we avoid cue sticks and come to an agreement: the future's not written to make the roses bloom. Who needs a country when you can have an island? I remember the unrevised Reagan, Fawn Hall and Contras, when the rich knew their place and didn't slum. What happened to the silver promises of childhood? The future we assumed belonged to everyone? We'll stay here all night until the doors close, until the sun rises and the streets guide us toward sleep, if that's what it takes to solve the mystery.

The Persian Aub Zam-Zam Club

There are rules I won't follow: take a seat, bills on the bar, order a dry martini. Ladies receive napkins. Bruno might serve punks in spikes while suits get shown the door. He says the city's gone to hell: women used to wear white gloves. Rubbing dust off a bottle: "You can have a Budweiser," he says, "it's the worst beer brewed in America." The glasses are polished like soldiers, gleam like the eye of an earnest young man who once fought the Japanese. What Bruno wants now is for you to follow orders. He fought overseas, served his country. What on earth have you ever done?

The Owl Tree

Bobby's either drunk or pouring drinks behind the bar, blending another martini, keeping an eye on the clientele, extending an invitation *to go upstairs*. Bobby prefers to watch, like the owls that clutter every wall. Owl clocks, owl mirrors. *Drunk as an owl*, the saying's lost. For now, he's half in love with James, the waiter who serves with schooled formality, props Bobby into place, and keeps the damn hookers on the street.

Burial Fragments

—Buena Vista Park

There's no room for the dead

in this small city, nearly an island,
where we trade corpses for houses

digging up graves
and disturbing the bones.

You can die in San Francisco,
but you can't keep the real estate.

On a path toward the hospital,
gutters laid from headstones,

names split from dates.
I visit to read fragments,

cursive of another century
spelling out a memory:

Frances, loving Mother.
Many names I'll never find.

They were turned to face the earth.

Not Far Underground

I held my breath
for the first trip back
since the panic attacks, when I pushed
the whoo-whoo button
and went phobic. My eyes locked
on a ticket-taker stuck in her chamber
like a fortuneteller. The future?
That's a one-way train.
Pay your fare and go where you like:
you can ride all night with no destination.

The city had grown ugly
in my absence. No one looked ballroom—
there was no spinning across the floor
in subway light. And the smell
of piss-stained corners
no longer proved a comedy.
I wasn't twenty-four
and laughing all the way
at the double-take man:

Having a trip, having a trip?
Acid or weed, acid or weed?

Flipped a turnstile, shuffled downstairs
and the walls and my lungs
didn't collapse. Imagine that?
If we were seated together
you wouldn't have known
a thing was wrong.

Shot through the tube
like an experiment. Got off—
released and rushed
giddy into evening, an easy walk
toward home and only once
looked over my shoulder.

II.

Russian Winters

Yvonne learned to speak Russian
after childbirth, her newborn sucking milk
while she practiced the vowels of Pushkin—

a language of gutturals, opposition to winter.

Today there's a threat of rain
and too many ripe oranges
left unpicked in the yards of Palo Alto,

once orchards. I miss the days I never knew

when the houses were trees
and the valley in winter
looked like snowfall from the blossoms.

Whatever I thought of her must have been partial.

Her husband died of cancer.
She faced her struggles, of which I knew nothing.
Pushkin wrote: *the years are fleeting,*

someone's hour is already at hand.

Tremble House

When I walk the leafy alley, I don't remember where I lived, can't find the door I once passed through where Jeffrey roomed with his orange coffee mug and orange shirt because someone he once loved loved orange. The walls were filled with nudes and abstract genitalia. I found myself the straight one, summer roommate in a spacious house where a bougainvillea erupted into a Mexican dress. I stole *Alice in Wonderland* and grew smaller. Her advice: enter a house listening, arrive like a gift. Jeffrey kept quiet about love, a way of sharing privacies. When my girlfriend visited on weekends, we proceeded with caution, as if our sex might wake his memory of the dead.

Flowers and Runaways

Street teens repeat the standard line: *Spare change for bud?* Who sleeps in a park, who sleeps in a suburb, the shirt's the same: *Green Day*. You lived at Haight and Ashbury, the house without a gate, and stepped over junkies sprawled on a welcome mat, gloving your hand to retrieve their needles. Sunday mornings, hung over, you slipped out to buy coffee and bagels, to breathe the park air and soak up the fog, its democratic calm, what you shared with those teens besides the angel's trumpets, pendulous bell that calls an eye to see and a mouth to taste its poison.

Infant Phrenology

Hello, world. Hello, animal.
Here's the real *undinal vast belly*:
fortuneteller's ball concealing
our future: womb-stranger.
The bundle, the bun, the solved equation.
The medicine, the talcum, the miconium.
Mind the fontanel. The smallest hand
built for your hand. The magic number
turning the couplet into three, solid
as the legs of a milking stool.
Birth prepares a face for the breast:
nose pushed up, tongue untied,
testing your weather for a nipple.
His mouth cries and just like that
it's laughter. Soundings meant
for you alone to hear. Baby things.
The songs we never thought we'd sing.

Birthmark

The mark that means your mother wished for wine,
spilled across a cheek like the boot of Italy.

The spot that says she tasted beets. Smashed apple.
Stork nip, angel spit. A stain there to remind us:

we're made of blood. Scar of a prior life.
Blemish (v.): *to shine, flash, burn*. Did she crave strawberries,

startle and touch her face? Did she stare at mice?
A finger pressed to her temple when the moon

passed before the sun. Demon sign, sign of fortune:
on the left cheek, ruin, on the right, a happy marriage.

Child-Rearing

In the days of first breath, the newborn breeds a rash and since the fact of parenthood is now permanent you phone your mother for advice, a gift you think you're giving of her own expertise, a chance to take part, but when she claims she's got no idea what to do, can't recall that was nearly forty years ago, and if she could remember now what she did for your skin no doubt today the medicine would be different, totally opposed, even, to a cream she might have applied with such care, back then, leaning over the crib and no real grave concern.

Boy

He mimics. And drinks ungodly volumes of milk.
Again, again
he cries to hear the book about a dog who plays flute,
laughing like a drunk at jokes he doesn't get.

He overhears the rain like a conversation
and murmurs to himself, not like a lonely man,
but one amused by genius. He doesn't know
heaven or death. Too young to spot hummingbirds,

too old to swaddle like a mummy.
Words appear in his mouth from the air.
He's got no reason to believe
a dog can't speak.

Early Stages

—for the new parents

Here comes the red wagon
loaded with tears— you can't
say *tears* but you're not deaf
and so you'll hear tears
waterboarding your heart
in the hours you once called
the drunkest but you're sober
as a map your steady hand
ready to sail the ship to calm.
Here comes the lightning,
here comes the lullaby jazz.
If you ever try to steal away,
the child's spirit, a mixture
of kerosene and laughter,
follows you to the dark side
of the bar where hustlers wait
with urgy stories to share
about their parents, dear old
Mom and Dad, and the awful things,
once upon a time, they did to them.

Polar Bear Express

The boy won't fall asleep
without books, pictures
before bed of polar bears
who never leave a scent
of blood against the ice,
watered down tales of jolly
rotten pirates setting sail.
The cannons shoot coconuts.
If there's a pistol, it's polished,
and never pointed at a slave.
A hand. A shove. Scarred knees,
written report. *She pushed me first.*
Every night I read with attention—
skipping over *soldiers* and *kill*.
I censor. I form a human shield.
I leave whole cities unburned.

Imaginary Child

When I ask my five-year-old about infinity
he pauses from a puzzle
long enough to say, *My sister's waiting there.*

•

In one version of the story, we split—
she wants to try again for a daughter;
I admit to an irrational fear of twins
and can't decide if the proposed girl
exists as a gift of light made flesh
or a pile of laundry and tears.

•

We should have started earlier.
We should have had another child.

•

Once you add a line, the triangle
turns square.

She could have perfected my scowl,
spent hours on the living room floor

drawing the proverbial unicorn.
Nicknames drift into space—

Shaggy Pants, Curly Button, Puddle Whump.
I'm too old for milk and puke

fists of hair and *why won't anyone*
in this house just put on their clothes?

Knock-kneed jitterbug, balloon enthusiast,
one quick scrawl across a vacant lot.

•

No daughter to divide the last effects.

That's not fair, that's not fair.

He will miss her more than us.

III.

Children's Notebook

My mother's oxygen tank, the way she hides hammers

•

Thinks he's a *billionaire* the smartest man
dancing on the planet his wife sleeping
with the neighbor and what was your name again?

•

Like a winter fly
          no one likes
he keeps living

•

Little girl, rose still in hand, found in coffin beneath San Francisco home
                    —San Francisco Chronicle

Two windows to watch heaven approach.
A rose in hand, still red, flowers tied to the grass of her hair.

What got her, what gets us.

In the disinterred casket, the white lace of her dress.

And you thought nothing lasts these days.

Over her heart, a cross of lavender.
                              Eucalyptus leaves
laid by her side, which would've been
                              new to California.

A name given to her. Miranda. A name like an island.

What about Ophelia?

All breath just disappearing.

•

We rehearse the dinners of childhood—

one prefers to lie on the floor (bad back).

One keeps a spacious office where I'd like to reside.
Japanese screens, a sense below the calamity, of calm.

Or, a former parlor where Edwardians once sat out summers
and spoke in codes that gave us Freud.

A stuffed couch where I sit (and never lie down).

•

New Year's Day—
            clear skies
and sparrows telling stories

•

Today my son spies
sidewalk Christmas trees
left for pulp in January—

faint smell of pine.
I trudge; he slumps.
School's in session.

Our winter holiday
becomes a melancholy past
while I carry lunch

and he readies his body
for today's lesson
on weightlessness in space.

•

Another year gone—
        I've hidden the gray hair
from my parents

•

Paper Movies: Periodic Table

A teacher's wooden pointer in hand (dirty newsreel print) she identifies elements you can't read, not yet fathoming the universe is dot-to-dot. The night sky's nothing more than an equation that makes you laugh — math is teeter-totter. Hold tight, Swing-Zilla, the alphabet's got teeth chewing into shoes that haven't left your feet. Master of Charts, you keep schedule and the train's on-time bursting through strontium, now you're the engineer watching out for monkeys who shoot arrows. One skewers your conductor's cap. Now you're bald. Now just look who's gotten old.

•

Or, the child's left ignored—
painting meticulous rainbows

while his mother organizes
lists for trips and untried recipes.

His father remembers earlier days
of bookstore jaunts when it was easy

to find cheap copies
of *The Women at Point Sur*

left unread because the violence
didn't match the beauty of its scenery—

cypresses blown inland
by fierce, mindless winds.

•

Shirrrr and *shirrrr* of a white noise machine.
Yes, it is comforting.

•

I sift through drawings
and ditch failed sketches,

keep the ones whose titles
I like best: *Imaginary Popsicles*

and a series of sea turtles
floating gently out to sea.

What does it mean, *father*?

Modern bob, triangle nose—
a portrait of his mother.

The train's in-progress, fashioned
in great detail with silver tracks

laid out heading west, disappearing
toward a white distance

neither one of us can imagine.

●

I need to find a place to keep
my father from my mother.

The patients take their steps
gingerly, skaters new to ice—

or actors assigned unspeaking parts, extras
in a staging of *One Flew Over the Cuckoo's Nest*.

Too elaborate? Call them the living dead.

She's still pretty and reaches out to hold
my son's hand, while the man

who's come to watch the tank
of fish who do just fine
                              without memory
tousles my boy's hair.

●

*I'd like to pass
          straight from dreams—
buried in cherry blossoms*

•

Let the boy feast
mother's away.
Let the boy feast on peaches
mother's away.

•

I watch for signs of breath.
He's easy in sleep—maybe I'm doing something right.

•

Beneath our city street, there's a river.

Where I hope to find its mouth,
the body's buried. No children

bring it calla lilies or sing songs
the river loved, ones without words,
murmur of water over stone.

No grass along the shore—
in the reeds no children
playing games devised by herons.

Once the river carried sky to ocean,
passing clouds, errant pelicans
perched on its shoulder. The river one long spell
no one thought could be broken.

Now the child makes a list of animals
he can no longer see—
long-snout alligator, ghost moth . . .

•

A was an animal, teeth and claw
B was a birdman, tweet and caw

•

Now that curiosity's broken
the seal and modern air
                            fills the casket,
she'll start to decay. Miranda
(still sad about her?) will die again.

•

The novelty of my father's illness
wears off—I visit when I want
and bring the boy and tiptoe
around any talk of dementia.

When it's time for us to leave,
the weekend manager, Ben,
gives a code, *Don't forget the code*
and I tap it out to open the gate

keeping in the crafty patients
and return, smell of sunlight,
musk of oak—
to another California summer.

•

Behind the fence—
          look!
violets in bloom

•

Job Post:

Into mourning? Down with the nearly dead?
A memory care unit may be right for you . . . .

•

I buy my son a wrestler's mask,
lucha libre, watch his stance
and scowl like foul weather lightning
ready to strike my aging body with *more*
and *more* and why can't I figure out
how to draw a dog just right?

•

An eraser, he's learned, leaves
a trace of branches behind—
ghost of a blossoming tree
he hadn't meant to draw.

•

The roomful of women and men
who look you in the eye and won't

remember you and you won't
remember them.

Come over—

let me brush away the crumbs
of death from your lips.

IV.

Lives I'll Never Live (for Minor White)

No one's fooled today by a handsome young man who distracts a camera from the scenery. Moonrise over coastal hills excuses the pose, a sailor on leave, rough jaw, anchor tattoo . . . nothing exists without skin. Contours of sandstone toned as a body, fissures in rock like lips, a male mouth. Close-ups reveal shape, not story: he couldn't tell us whose body he wanted and framed it again and again kneeling toward stone, lover over lover, catching how morning light pressed itself on water or revealed the wear of hands in an abandoned house. An open window, blurred hem of a coat, a man just disappearing. The great intent leaks through: God has lit the world on fire. Knowing he was dying, he turned the lens on himself, spry mystic dressed in rags, dressed in leather, one last chance to play the biker, the hippie, the Spirit of Death.

Explaining Wingrove

If I were gay, Wingrove said walking past the rainbow flags, *I could get laid here so fast*. We hadn't seen each other since his brother died. In high school, Wingrove called him *deviant*. There was a sheik from Dubai who fell in love, who promised riches. Limousines and champagne, last-minute flights to Rome. Then, suddenly, no one for the brother to touch. Fear of contagion, of who might talk. *Think that's bad?* Their father dies. Wingrove drops out to care for the one he hated so fiercely. And the shame he wants to explain: how it became easier. As his brother grew lighter, this is all he can say, a gesture that even now guides the body. *It became easier to lift him.*

*

In the script he's written, Wingrove plays the role of Intelligence spy. Leaving a post to dig deeper undercover, he investigates a plot that leads to the highest levels of authority. Wingrove adds a love interest, an old girlfriend newly divorced who welcomes the comfort he gives. *The other story*, he says, what he hasn't written yet, how at night when he returns home the audience watches his brother dying, neglected by everyone, how it's Wingrove alone who cares for him. In the morning, he showers, shaves, presses his shirt. Wingrove imagines whole scenes devoted to this, buttoning his cuffs, knotting his tie, leaning over the bed to kiss his brother goodbye.

*

Wingrove plays the horses. Studies jockeys, reads the betting line. Before a race, he canvases the pen to examine taped thoroughbred legs, flanks oily with sweat. Who's jittery today, who's taken sick? *Someone owes me.* Variations of this phrase: *I am owed, what I've been through.* Wingrove likes long shots; I place a minimum wager and choose my horse by its name, *Velocious.* At the race's start, no one watches closely, fingering their stubs. Only as the horses make the final turn do I learn how fast they run, the rider lifted off his seat, bent close to the neck, listening in for the final breaths.

Angelo's Hair Styling Salon & Electrolysis

From the barber's chair, I watch the same view: photographs of shirtless studs, Angelo in younger days hula dancing, my hair in the mirror that Angelo makes, for a time, less rinsed in gray. After a trim and the day's first gossip, he always turns the topic to Pierre, handsome neighbor who vanished to Palm Springs when his mother died and left the money and his clean-shaven looks. *Have you heard from Pierre?* Often we're the only ones left in the shop. We agree Elliot needs a woman before it's too late; but if he decides he's not straight, *he'll always find work as a house boy.* On quiet afternoons, I coax out stories of Tenderloin hookers whose hair Angelo bleached and bedside cuts for customers —wasted, confused, skeletal— who were dying of a new plague. *What's the first thing you notice on a woman?* Angelo asks then answers, *The teeth.* Evenings he devotes to the telenovelas: Pedro's in love with a little white witch; Pedro never falls in love with Tomás. Sundays he reserves for confession, Mission Dolores and the Bread of Christ. Says he lives alone; says he never dates. Like I'd tell anyone. Like I'd tell his mother.

Fascist Statue

On a red-eye, in turbulence,
I soothed a woman's nerves
whose conversation revealed
a cousin owned the mansion
I'd walked past for years—

hilltop vista, front yard so rare
in San Francisco. I imagined
wealth in decay
beneath splintered shingles,
ceilings stained by candle smoke,
shelves of Thackeray and Trollope.

Over a fountain that never held water,
a bronze statue of a winged goddess
releases a phalanx of birds.
Who owned it? Patriarchs with goldmines,
mad as mercury. The statue arrived
in better times, the woman said, a gift
from that poor man, Mussolini.

Target Practice

A Sunday morning voice
behind the door I'd just opened
said she was selling
the *Socialist Review*

and asked if I wasn't ready
to take up arms for the revolution.
I offered a dollar
and the conversation turned

to capitalism: she worked
part-time, didn't vote, and spent
her afternoons on the firing range
taking practice shots

at President Clinton.
I'd never held a handgun,
and she wanted me to learn.
The workers were uniting,

but I wanted coffee and the paper,
no matter what my comrade said.
I don't believe in revolution,
but I often want to let the stranger in.

Safelight

—Point Reyes Beach

My father measures the light
        and disappears beneath a cape
where he photographs a slogan

I can't begin to fathom:
        We Deserve the Bomb
spray-painted on a salt-rusted

VW bus stalled in sand, awash
        in fog. Surf punks
gone to float their luck against a riptide.

I'm waiting out the Reagan years
        with a man who reveres
thrift and industry, who believes in

museum scenes of dust bowl squalor:
        unplowed, unplanted, children
becoming dirt mothers hope not to bury.

Where calla lilies burst out, bouquets
        gather for a pine box casket. In the eye
of Walker Evans, four men occupy a platform,

no train in the yard, no train coming.
        Patterns of migration in a vacant scene:
tin roofs and telegraph wires, wooden planks

on a dock without cargo. Steel tracks curve
        toward the barren certainty of other towns,
the distance, like the future, out-of-focus—

the picture taken as if from a train
        leaving this town for good. Under safelight,
he shows me how to expose the print.

Color photographs of coastal fog develop
        black-and-white. In the perfect dark
we talk while the waves appear before us

of the men my father admires, steady-eyed
        gazers like Ralph Eugene Meatyard
the one he loves for the sound of his name.

End Days

My father's a dying organism
who once believed in perfection:
save your money, avoid lawyers.
Polonius at the breakfast table:
Neither a borrower nor a lender . . .
The democratic sky was always falling—
now he can't add, multiply or divide.
Inward: grief. Outward: rage.
Somewhere a market's falling,
slogans flare across a tickertape:
all boats rise and fall with the tide
of a mind that's pulling back each day.
Barb, he says, *what did I used to do*
when I worked? A clever young man,
a flying ace, one marvelous engineer
who failed to understand on summer trips
why we couldn't leave the sand at the beach.

Explaining Shockley

—father of the transistor (1910-1989)

When Shockley died, his children learned the news from the papers. Students burned his car when he lectured on race. He passed in infamy, alone except for Emmy, the widow my father once spied passing like a specter through the arches of an exclusive university, proof of a brush with greatness. Shockley's invention: our future. Transistors my father fabricated like elaborate microscopic cities. Now the book he wrote has turned obsolete. When I lift it off a shelf, the weight's more than paper and millboard. A dedication stays current, nearly the only words among schematics and equations: *To my long-suffering wife and oft-neglected children.* What he wanted to escape, the ice of Buffalo winters, a drafty bedroom where he listened to *The Shadow* by the hum of vacuum tubes and learned that famous saying: *Who knows what evil lurks in the hearts of men?*

Electronic News: Nagasaki

Through black-rimmed spectacles
        where he can't contaminate, behind glass,
my father watches a room of women

capped and goggled in lab gowns
        stitching together circuit boards.
He won't be touched.

The women stare through microscopes
        at fine grains of transistors, testing purity.
Their mothers and fathers farmed rice.

The monument, a melted pocket watch.
        A photograph of a man without hands.
Afterwards, he'll spot an udon shack

        and make the waitress understand: *Hai*
he wants soup, but *onegai*,
        without the raw white light of the egg.

Bhopal

Narayan told me about the city in India where he once studied, a literary centre known for festivals and lively debates, crowds gathering to hear the poetry readings which, he bragged, *went on forever*. But when he spoke the name, my face must have shifted. *Yes*, he said, *you've heard about the gas leak*. In December, clouds covered the city and its lakes. Warnings sounded and he walked uphill to find a place above the clouds, passing many who didn't know better than to take deep breaths, because the toxins left them short of breath, drawing in the yellow poison. I didn't ask whom he'd lost among the dead. He kept apologizing, embarrassed, repeating a story I'd heard before. All he wanted to tell me, he said, was that wherever you went today it seemed like no one read anymore.

Midnight Alley Fire

Smell of wax   vaguely sacred scent
my son says *candles*   spots wavering shadows
gestures of puppet theater: flames

twitch and snip as elders conspiring
before church. I pulled an alarm; it rang
like we'd won—a colony of birds sang

with lungs of brass. Sirens wailed
much to the boy's delight. Fire trucks
arrived bearing a lighted ladder—

like they didn't want to miss his birthday.
We hurried across the empty street
watching the apartment not burn.

Room to room heroes dragged hoses
checking for children of flame.
A smell of last rites quieted our days.

Ash if you touched it left marks of penitence.
Almost pillowed and sheeted in black
carcinogens, he's free for tomorrows

of boutonnières and heartache   free to hate us
free for joy   rent and the common
unspeakable lusts   we are permitted.

Morning boredoms.   The wrong of it all.
Learning how to count past twenty.

In Which White Horses Appear

Through the tunnel on a line that ends at the beach, ends in fog, the car never empty, students and secretaries, an elderly Chinese woman hauling greens. No seat so you'd stand, quiet even there in the bodily rush. Streets tripped by and you picked up the alphabet, *Quintara, Rivera*. The ocean before you shimmered into place. Those were the first days, and this seemed like the new world, promised all along. The city so close to its psychedelic glaze you caught a contact high. No one tipped you off as two white horses appeared beyond the window, their own hallucination, coats of cream, coats of fog, there as long as you were, and gone now, long gone.

The End

Fire, yes. Then, a peace of angels.

Believers pay a price to lift the veil.

Poof: the future. Celestials on earth.

The soul unhoused becomes light.

You hardly notice it dancing through the trees.

Would the living ever think about the dead?

The dead condemned by their disbelief?

And wouldn't this leave hatred in their world?

Better to keep these stirrings interior and welcome

insects a child studies through glass

little demons toiling   scurriers in search of seed.

ACKNOWLEDGEMENTS

Many thanks to the editors and staff of the following journals in which these poems first appeared.

Anacapa Review: "Blam-Blam" and "Child-Rearing"

Blackbird: "Electronic News: Nagasaki," "Explaining Shockley," "Russian Winters," and "Not Far Underground"

Crazyhorse: "Projection"

European Journal of International Law: "Bhopal"

Great River Review: "End Days," "Early Stages," "Midnight Alley Fire"

Meridian: "Stroller" and "Boy"

Natural Bridge: "Birthmark"

Poetry Northwest: "Infant Phrenology"

Ploughshares: "Polar Bear Express" and "Threat Level"

The Cincinnati Review: "Burial Fragments," "Angelo's Hair Stying Salon & Electrolysis"

The Kenyon Review: "Into the City," "Explaining Wingrove," "Lives I'll Never Live," "The End," and "In Which White Horses Appear"

The San Francisco Chronicle: "Fascist Statue"

The Southern Review: "Target Practice" and "Flowers and Runaways"

Third Coast: "Imaginary Child"

Waccamaw: "The Shape of Conversation at The Gold Cane"

Washington Square: "Safelight"

White Wall Review: "Tremble House"

"Memorial" (as "On Mission Street") appeared in *99 Poems for the 99 Percent: An Anthology of Poetry* (99: The Press, 2014).

Special thanks to the Stanford Creative Writing Program for the gifts of time and community which made completion of this manuscript possible. Thanks to Michael Collier, Jen Grotz, and Noreen Cargill of the Bread Loaf

Writers' Conference for fellowship and support along the way.

My deepest gratitude to the faculty, staff, and students of the Warren Wilson MFA Program for Writers, without whom this book would not have taken form. In particular, I'd like to acknowledge my teachers Brooks Haxton, Alan Williamson, Reginald Gibbons, Debra Allbery, Alan Shapiro, and the generous vision of Ellen Bryant Voigt.

For their criticism and readerly patience, I'd like to thank Maria Hummel, Alexandra Teague, Rita Mae Reese, and Sara Michas-Martin (the Mission Pie group) along with Christian Gullette, David Roderick, Bruce Snider, Rebecca Black, and Dean Rader. For their on-going support and example, I thank Eavan Boland, Kenneth Fields, and W.S. Di Piero. Thank you to Carole Marcus for listening and remembering. And thanks to my parents and family for providing a good home for books. Lastly, I'd like to thank Robin Ekiss, who turns prose into poetry on a daily basis.

About the Poet

Keith Ekiss is a former Wallace Stegner Fellow in Poetry at Stanford University. He is the author of *Pima Road Notebook* (New Issues Poetry & Prose, 2010) and translator of *The Fire's Journey* (Tavern Books, 2019), an epic poem by the Costa Rican writer Eunice Odio in four volumes. *Territory of Dawn: The Selected Poems of Eunice Odio* was published in Spring, 2016 by The Bitter Oleander Press. He is the past recipient of fellowships and residencies from the Bread Loaf Writers' Conference, Community of Writers' Conference, Millay Colony for the Arts, Santa Fe Art Institute, and the Petrified Forest National Park.

Barry Spacks
Poetry Prize Winners

Burial Fragments
Poems by Keith Ekiss

Dear Empire
Poems by Holly Karapetkova

In the Cathedral of My Undoing
Poems by Kellam Ayres

Accidental Garden
Poems by Catherine Esposito Prescott

Like All Light
Poems by Todd Copeland

Curriculum
Poems by Meghan Dunn

Drinking with O'Hara
Poems by Glenn Freeman

The Ghosts of Lost Animals
Poems by Michelle Bonczek Evory

Posthumous Noon
Poems by Aaron Baker

Burning Down Disneyland
Poems by Kurt Olsson

Instead of Sadness
Poems by Catherine Abbey Hodges

ALSO FROM
GUNPOWDER PRESS

Learning to Drown, poems by SM Stubbs

Empty Me Full, poems by Catherine Abbey Hodges

Frangible Operas, poems by Susan Kelly-DeWitt

Before Traveling to Alabama, poems by David Case

Mother Lode, poems by Peg Quinn

Raft of Days, poems by Catherine Abbey Hodges

Unfinished City, poems by Nan Cohen

Original Face, poems by Jim Peterson

Shaping Water, poems by Barry Spacks

The Tarnation of Faust, poems by David Case

Mouth & Fruit, poems by Chryss Yost

JOHN RIDLAND POETRY PRIZE

Sad Animal, poems by Joshua McKinney

DRYDEN-VREELAND BOOK PRIZE

Three-Day Weekend, poems by Christopher Blackman

FULL CATALOG AT GUNPOWDERPRESS.COM